Keeping Children Safe in Education

Statutory guidance for schools and colleges

To purchase a copy please visit:

www.TheNationalCurriculum.com

or scan this code to take you there:

Contents

Summary

About this guidance

This is statutory guidance from the Department for Education issued under Section 175, Education Act 2002, the Education (Independent School Standards) (England) Regulations 2010 as amended by SI 2012/2962 and the Education (Non-Maintained Special Schools) (England) Regulations 2011. Schools and colleges must have regard to it when carrying out their duties to safeguard and promote the welfare of children.

Unless otherwise specified, 'school' means all schools whether maintained, non-maintained or independent schools, including academies and free schools, alternative provision academies and pupil referral units. 'School' does not include maintained nursery schools. 'College' means further education colleges and sixth-form colleges, and relates to children under the age of 18, but excludes 16-19 academies and free schools (which are required to comply with relevant safeguarding legislation by virtue of their funding agreement).

This document contains information on what schools and colleges **should** do and sets out the legal duties with which schools and colleges **must** comply. It should be read alongside <u>Working Together to Safeguard Children 2013</u> which applies to all the schools referred to above, including maintained nursery schools.

Legislation this guidance refers to is listed at Annex A.

Who this guidance is for

- Governing bodies of maintained schools and colleges, proprietors of independent schools (including academies, free schools and alternative provision academies) and management committees of pupil referral units (PRUs), further education colleges and sixth form colleges.

- Staff in all schools and colleges; the above persons should ensure that **all staff read at least part one.**

What it replaces

This guidance replaces *Safeguarding Children and Safer Recruitment in Education* (December 2006).

Part one: Safeguarding information for all staff

What school and college staff should know and do

1. Safeguarding and promoting the welfare of children is defined for the purposes of this guidance as: protecting children from maltreatment; preventing impairment of children's health or development; ensuring that children grow up in circumstances consistent with the provision of safe and effective care; and taking action to enable all children to have the best outcomes.

2. Children includes everyone under the age of 18.

3. Where a child is suffering significant harm, or is likely to do so, action should be taken to protect that child.[1] Action should also be taken to promote the welfare of a child in need of additional support, even if they are not suffering harm or are at immediate risk.[2]

The role of the school or college

4. Everyone who comes into contact with children and their families has a role to play in safeguarding children. School and college staff are particularly important as they are in a position to identify concerns early and provide help for children, to prevent concerns from escalating. Schools and colleges and their staff form part of the wider safeguarding system for children. This system is described in statutory guidance *Working Together to Safeguard Children 2013*.[3] Schools and colleges should work with social care, the police, health services and other services to promote the welfare of children and protect them from harm.

5. Each school and college should have a designated safeguarding lead who will provide support to staff members to carry out their safeguarding duties and who will liaise closely with other services such as children's social care.

The role of school and college staff

6. The *Teacher Standards 2012*[4] state that teachers, including headteachers, should safeguard children's wellbeing and maintain public trust in the teaching profession as part of their professional duties.

---

[1] Such action might be taken under section 47 and section 44 of the Children Act 1989.
[2] Such action might be taken under section 17 of the Children Act 1989.
[3] Department for Education guidance: Working Together to Safeguard Children 2013
[4] The Teachers' Standards apply to: trainees working towards QTS; all teachers completing their statutory induction period (newly qualified teachers [NQTs]); and teachers in maintained schools, including maintained special schools, who are covered by the 2012 appraisal regulations.

7.   All school and college staff have a responsibility to provide a safe environment in which children can learn.

8.   All school and college staff have a responsibility to identify children who may be in need of extra help or who are suffering, or are likely to suffer, significant harm. All staff then have a responsibility to take appropriate action, working with other services as needed.

9.   In addition to working with the designated safeguarding lead staff members should be aware that they may be asked to support social workers to take decisions about individual children.

What school and college staff need to know

10.   All staff members should be aware of systems within their school or college which support safeguarding and these should be explained to them as part of staff induction. This includes: the school's or college's child protection policy; the school's or college's staff behaviour policy (sometimes called a code of conduct); and the designated safeguarding lead.

11.   All staff members should also receive appropriate child protection training which is regularly updated.

What school and college staff should look out for

12.   All school and college staff members should be aware of the signs of abuse and neglect so that they are able to identify cases of children who may be in need of help or protection.

13.   Staff members working with children are advised to maintain an attitude of 'it could happen here' where safeguarding is concerned. When concerned about the welfare of a child, staff members should always act in the interests of the child.

14.   There are various expert sources of advice on the signs of abuse and neglect. Each area's Local Safeguarding Children Board (LSCB) should be able to advise on useful material, including training options. One good source of advice is provided on the NSPCC website. Types of abuse and neglect, and examples of specific safeguarding issues, are described in paragraphs 20-25.[5]

15.   Knowing what to look for is vital to the early identification of abuse and neglect. If staff members are unsure they should always speak to children's social care.

16.   A child going missing from an education setting is a potential indicator of abuse or neglect. School and college staff members should follow their procedures for dealing with

---

[5] Department for Education (DfE) training materials on neglect

5

children who go missing, particularly on repeat occasions. They should act to identify any risk of abuse and neglect, including sexual abuse or exploitation. More information can be found in this guidance about children who run away or go missing from home or care

What school and college staff should do if they have concerns about a child

17.   If staff members have concerns about a child they should raise these with the school's or college's designated safeguarding lead. This also includes situations of abuse which may involve staff members. The safeguarding lead will usually decide whether to make a referral to children's social care, but it is important to note that any staff member can refer their concerns to children's social care directly.[6] Where a child and family would benefit from co-ordinated support from more than one agency (for example education, health, housing, police) there should be an inter-agency assessment. These assessments should identify what help the child and family require to prevent needs escalating to a point where intervention would be needed via a statutory assessment under the Children Act 1989. The early help assessment should be undertaken by a lead professional who could be a teacher, special educational needs co-ordinator, General Practitioner (GP), family support worker, and/or health visitor.

18.   **If, at any point, there is a risk of immediate serious harm to a child a referral should be made to children's social care immediately. Anybody can make a referral. If the child's situation does not appear to be improving the staff member with concerns should press for re-consideration. Concerns should always lead to help for the child at some point.**

19.   It is important for children to receive the right help at the right time to address risks and prevent issues escalating. Research and Serious Case Reviews have repeatedly shown the dangers of failing to take effective action. Poor practice includes: failing to act on and refer the early signs of abuse and neglect, poor record keeping, failing to listen to the views of the child, failing to re-assess concerns when situations do not improve, sharing information too slowly and a lack of challenge to those who appear not to be taking action.[7]

---

[6] Advice on whistleblowing can be found on GOV.UK
[7] Brandon et al, Learning from Serious Case Reviews (SCRs) 2011

Action when a child has suffered or is likely to suffer harm

This diagram illustrates what action should be taken and who should take it when there are concerns about a child. If, at any point, there is a risk of immediate serious harm to a child a referral should be made to children's social care immediately. **Anybody can make a referral.**

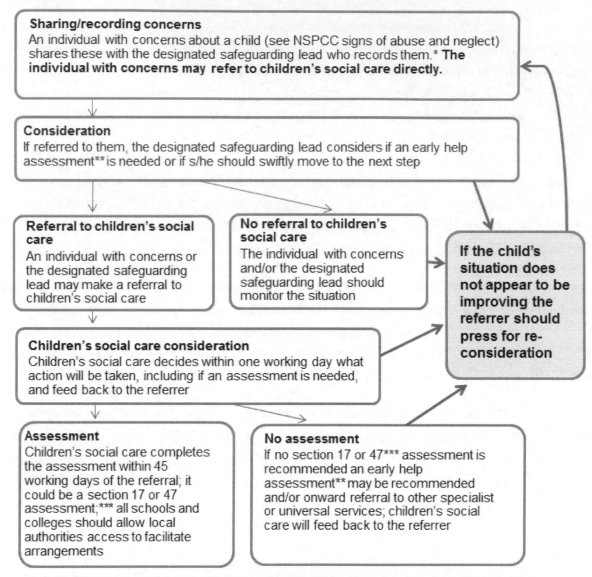

Sharing/recording concerns
An individual with concerns about a child (see NSPCC signs of abuse and neglect) shares these with the designated safeguarding lead who records them.* **The individual with concerns may refer to children's social care directly.**

Consideration
If referred to them, the designated safeguarding lead considers if an early help assessment** is needed or if s/he should swiftly move to the next step

Referral to children's social care
An individual with concerns or the designated safeguarding lead may make a referral to children's social care

No referral to children's social care
The individual with concerns and/or the designated safeguarding lead should monitor the situation

If the child's situation does not appear to be improving the referrer should press for re-consideration

Children's social care consideration
Children's social care decides within one working day what action will be taken, including if an assessment is needed, and feed back to the referrer

Assessment
Children's social care completes the assessment within 45 working days of the referral; it could be a section 17 or 47 assessment;*** all schools and colleges should allow local authorities access to facilitate arrangements

No assessment
If no section 17 or 47*** assessment is recommended an early help assessment** may be recommended and/or onward referral to other specialist or universal services; children's social care will feed back to the referrer

* In cases which also involve an allegation of abuse against a staff member, see part four of this guidance which explains action the school or college should take in respect of the staff member

** Where a child and family would benefit from coordinated support from more than one agency (eg, education, health, housing, police) there should be an inter-agency assessment. These assessments should identify what help the child and family require to prevent needs escalating to a point where intervention would be needed via a statutory assessment under the Children Act 1989. The early help assessment should be undertaken by a lead professional who could be a teacher, special educational needs coordinator, General Practitioner (GP), family support worker, and/or health visitor.

*** Where there are more complex needs, help may be provided under section 17 of the Children Act 1989 (children in need). Where there are child protection concerns local authority services must make enquiries and decide if any action must be taken under section 47 of the Children Act 1989.

Types of abuse and neglect

20.   **Abuse**: a form of maltreatment of a child. Somebody may abuse or neglect a child by inflicting harm, or by failing to act to prevent harm. They may be abused by an adult or adults or another child or children.

21.   **Physical abuse**: a form of abuse which may involve hitting, shaking, throwing, poisoning, burning or scalding, drowning, suffocating or otherwise causing physical harm to a child. Physical harm may also be caused when a parent or carer fabricates the symptoms of, or deliberately induces, illness in a child.

22.   **Emotional abuse**: the persistent emotional maltreatment of a child such as to cause severe and adverse effects on the child's emotional development. It may involve conveying to a child that they are worthless or unloved, inadequate, or valued only insofar as they meet the needs of another person. It may include not giving the child opportunities to express their views, deliberately silencing them or 'making fun' of what they say or how they communicate. It may feature age or developmentally inappropriate expectations being imposed on children. These may include interactions that are beyond a child's developmental capability as well as overprotection and limitation of exploration and learning, or preventing the child participating in normal social interaction. It may involve seeing or hearing the ill-treatment of another. It may involve serious bullying (including cyberbullying), causing children frequently to feel frightened or in danger, or the exploitation or corruption of children. Some level of emotional abuse is involved in all types of maltreatment of a child, although it may occur alone.

23.   **Sexual abuse**: involves forcing or enticing a child or young person to take part in sexual activities, not necessarily involving a high level of violence, whether or not the child is aware of what is happening. The activities may involve physical contact, including assault by penetration (for example rape or oral sex) or non-penetrative acts such as masturbation, kissing, rubbing and touching outside of clothing. They may also include non-contact activities, such as involving children in looking at, or in the production of, sexual images, watching sexual activities, encouraging children to behave in sexually inappropriate ways, or grooming a child in preparation for abuse (including via the internet). Sexual abuse is not solely perpetrated by adult males. Women can also commit acts of sexual abuse, as can other children.

24.   **Neglect**: the persistent failure to meet a child's basic physical and/or psychological needs, likely to result in the serious impairment of the child's health or development. Neglect may occur during pregnancy as a result of maternal substance abuse. Once a child is born, neglect may involve a parent or carer failing to: provide adequate food, clothing and shelter (including exclusion from home or abandonment); protect a child from physical and emotional harm or danger; ensure adequate supervision (including the use of inadequate care-givers); or ensure access to appropriate medical care or treatment. It may also include neglect of, or unresponsiveness to, a child's basic emotional needs.

Specific safeguarding issues

25.　　Expert and professional organisations are best placed to provide up-to-date guidance and practical support on specific safeguarding issues. For example NSPCC offers information for schools and colleges on the TES website and also on its own website www.nspcc.org.uk Schools and colleges can also access broad government guidance on the issues listed below via the GOV.UK website:

- child sexual exploitation (CSE) – see also below

- bullying including cyberbullying

- domestic violence

- drugs

- fabricated or induced illness

- faith abuse

- female genital mutilation (FGM) – see also below

- forced marriage

- gangs and youth violence

- gender-based violence/violence against women and girls (VAWG)

- mental health

- private fostering

- radicalisation

- sexting

- teenage relationship abuse

- trafficking

Further information on Child Sexual Exploitation and Female Genital Mutilation

Child sexual exploitation(CSE) involves exploitative situations, contexts and relationships where young people receive something (for example food, accommodation, drugs, alcohol, gifts, money or in some cases simply affection) as a result of engaging in sexual activities. Sexual exploitation can take many forms ranging from the seemingly 'consensual' relationship where sex is exchanged for affection or gifts, to serious organised crime by gangs and groups. What marks out exploitation is an imbalance of power in the relationship. The perpetrator always holds some kind of power over the victim which increases as the exploitative relationship develops. Sexual exploitation involves varying degrees of coercion, intimidation or enticement, including unwanted pressure from peers to have sex, sexual bullying including cyberbullying and grooming. However, it also important to recognise that some young people who are being sexually exploited do not exhibit any external signs of this abuse.

Female Genital Mutilation (FGM): professionals in all agencies, and individuals and groups in relevant communities, need to be alert to the possibility of a girl being at risk of FGM, or already having suffered FGM. There is a range of potential indicators that a child or young person may be at risk of FGM, which individually may not indicate risk but if there are two or more indicators present this could signal a risk to the child or young person. Victims of FGM are likely to come from a community that is known to practise FGM. Professionals should note that girls at risk of FGM may not yet be aware of the practice or that it may be conducted on them, so sensitivity should always be shown when approaching the subject. Warning signs that FGM may be about to take place, or may have already taken place, can be found on pages 11-12 of the Multi-Agency Practice Guidelines referred to previously. Staff should activate local safeguarding procedures, using existing national and local protocols for multi-agency liaison with police and children's social care.

Part two: The management of safeguarding

The responsibility of governing bodies and proprietors

26.   Governing bodies and proprietors must ensure that they comply with their duties under legislation. They must also have regard to this guidance to ensure that the policies, procedures and training in their schools or colleges are effective and comply with the law at all times.[8]

Inter-agency working

27.   Governing bodies and proprietors should ensure that the school or college contributes to inter-agency working in line with statutory guidance *Working Together to Safeguard Children 2013*. This includes providing a co-ordinated offer of early help when additional needs of children are identified and contributing to inter-agency plans to provide additional support to children subject to child protection plans. All schools and colleges should allow access for children's social care from the host local authority and, where appropriate, from a placing local authority, for that authority to conduct, or to consider whether to conduct, a section 17 or a section 47 assessment.[9]

28.   Governing bodies and proprietors of all schools and colleges should ensure that their safeguarding arrangements take into account the procedures and practice of the local authority as part of the inter-agency safeguarding procedures set up by the Local Safeguarding Children Board (LSCB). Section 10 of the Children Act 2004 requires a local authority to make arrangements to promote co-operation between itself and its relevant partners and other organisations who are engaged in activities relating to children.[10] Under section 14B of the Children Act 2004 the LSCB can require a school or college to supply information in order to perform its functions; this must be complied with.

29.   Governing bodies and proprietors should ensure a member of the governing

---

[8] Section 175 Education Act 2002 and the Education (Independent School Standards) (England) Regulations 2010, made under section 157 Education Act 2002. Colleges, non-maintained special schools and independent schools: the definition of 'children' applies to the statutory responsibilities for safeguarding and promoting the welfare of children ie, those under 18.

[9] Where a child has more complex needs, help may be provided under section 17 of the Children Act 1989 (children in need). Where there are child protection concerns local authority services must make enquiries and decide if any action must be taken under section 47 of the Children Act 1989.

[10] Applied to the management committee of pupil referral units through paragraph 20B of Schedule 1 to the Education (Pupil Referral Units) (Application of Enactment) (England) Regulations 2007. The relevant partners include maintained schools, non-maintained special schools, academies and free schools and colleges, which are under a duty to co-operate with the local authority in the making of such arrangements. The arrangements made by local authorities under section 10 may extend to other types of independent and non-maintained schools (ie, other than academies and free schools) as such schools engage in activities relating to children.

body, usually the chair, is nominated to liaise with the local authority and/or partner agencies on issues of child protection and in the event of allegations of abuse made against the headteacher, the principal of a college or proprietor or member of governing body of an independent school. In the event of allegations of abuse being made against the headteacher and/or where the headteacher is also the sole proprietor of an independent school, allegations should be reported directly to the local authority.

Safeguarding policies

30.   Governing bodies and proprietors should ensure there is an effective child protection policy in place together with a staff behaviour policy (code of conduct). Both should be provided to all staff – including temporary staff and volunteers – on induction. The child protection policy should describe procedures which are in accordance with government guidance and refer to locally agreed inter-agency procedures put in place by the LSCB, be updated annually, and be available publicly either via the school or college website or by other means.

31.   Headteachers and principals should ensure that the policies and procedures adopted by governing bodies and proprietors, particularly concerning referrals of cases of suspected abuse and neglect, are followed by all staff.

The designated safeguarding lead

32.   Governing bodies and proprietors should appoint a member of staff of the school's or college's leadership team to the role of designated safeguarding lead. This should be explicit in the role-holder's job description (see Annex B which describes the broad areas of responsibility). This person should have the appropriate authority and be given the time, funding, training, resources and support to provide advice and support to other staff on child welfare and child protection matters, to take part in strategy discussions and inter-agency meetings – and/or to support other staff to do so – and to contribute to the assessment of children.

33.   The designated safeguarding lead should liaise with the local authority and work with other agencies in line with *Working Together to Safeguard Children 2013*. There should always be cover for this role.

34.   **If, at any point, there is a risk of immediate serious harm to a child a referral should be made to children's social care immediately. Anybody can make a referral.**

35.   The designated safeguarding lead should undergo updated child protection training every two years. The headteacher and all staff members should undergo child protection training which is updated regularly, in line with advice from the LSCB.

Opportunities to teach safeguarding

36.   Governing bodies and proprietors should consider how children may be taught about safeguarding, including online, through teaching and learning opportunities, as part of providing a broad and balanced curriculum. This may include covering relevant issues through personal, social health and economic education (PSHE), and/or – for maintained schools and colleges – through sex and relationship education (SRE).

Inspection

37.   The assessment of the quality of leadership and management made during an Ofsted inspection includes an assessment of the effectiveness of the safeguarding arrangements in place in the school or college to ensure that there is safe recruitment and that all children are safe. The Ofsted handbook provides further information on what inspectors must do and what school and colleges can expect, and provides guidance for inspectors on making their judgements. Ofsted have also produced a handbook on the inspection of further education and skills. Inspections of independent schools will check that the Independent School Standard which concerns the welfare, health and safety of children is met.[11]

38.   In line with part three of this guidance, governing bodies and proprietors should prevent people who pose a risk of harm from working with children by adhering to statutory responsibilities to check staff who work with children, taking proportionate decisions on whether to ask for any checks beyond what is required; and ensuring volunteers are appropriately supervised. The school or college should have written recruitment and selection policies and procedures in place. The school staffing regulations require governing bodies of schools to ensure that at least one person on any appointment panel has undertaken safer recruitment training. Please see footnote for future arrangements.[12]

39.   In line with part four of this guidance, governing bodies and proprietors should ensure there are procedures in place to handle allegations against members of staff and volunteers. Such allegations should be referred to the Local Authority Designated Officer (LADO). There must also be procedures in place to make a referral to the Disclosure and Barring Service (DBS) if a person in regulated activity has been dismissed or removed

---

[11] Ofsted best practice reports for safeguarding in schools and best practice for safeguarding in colleges Office of the Children's Commissioner for England reports You have someone to trust – outstanding safeguarding practice in primary schools and Feeling safe, keeping safe: good practice in safeguarding and child protection in secondary schools

[12] School Staffing (England) Regulations 2009, regulation 9: at least one member of a recruitment panel must undertake safer recruitment training which, subject to parliamentary procedure, from September 2014 will no longer need to be provided by a person approved by the Secretary of State. Schools may choose appropriate training and may take advice from their LSCB in doing so. The training should cover, as a minimum, the content of this guidance.

due to safeguarding concerns, or would have been had they not resigned.[13] **This is a legal duty and failure to refer when the criteria are met is a criminal offence.**[14]

40.   Governing bodies and proprietors should also ensure that there are procedures in place to handle allegations against other children.

The child's wishes

41.   Governing bodies, proprietors and school or college leaders should ensure the child's wishes or feelings are taken into account when determining what action to take and what services to provide to protect individual children through ensuring there are systems in place for children to express their views and give feedback. Governing bodies and proprietors should ensure that staff members do not promise confidentiality to the child and always act in the interests of the child.

Boarding schools, children's home and host families

42.   Schools and colleges that offer residential accommodation should be particularly alert to children's safeguarding. Such schools and colleges should also be alert to pupil relationships and the potential for peer abuse particularly in schools and colleges with a significant gender imbalance. Considerations for such schools and colleges are set out in Annex C, which also covers issues where children stay with host families.

Looked after children

43.   Governing bodies must appoint a designated teacher to promote the educational achievement of children who are looked after and to ensure that this person has appropriate training.[15]

44.   The most common reason for children becoming looked after is as a result of abuse and/or neglect. Governing bodies and proprietors should ensure that staff have the skills, knowledge and understanding necessary to keeping looked after children safe. In particular, they should ensure that appropriate staff have the information they need in relation to a child's looked after legal status (whether they are looked after under voluntary arrangements with consent of parents or on an interim or full care order) and contact arrangements with birth parents or those with parental responsibility. They should also have information about the child's care arrangements and the levels of authority delegated to the carer by the authority looking after him/her. The designated safeguarding lead, through the designated teacher[16] for looked after children, should have details of the child's social worker and the name of the virtual school head in the

---

[13] Safeguarding Vulnerable Groups Act 2006, Section 35.

[14] Safeguarding Vulnerable Groups Act 2006, Section 38.

[15] The Children and Young Person's Act 2008. This legislation and accompanying statutory guidance on the role of designated teachers applies to academies through their funding agreements.

[16] Department for Education – Guidance about designated teacher for looked after children

authority that looks after the child.[17]

Missing children

45.   A child going missing from an education setting is a potential indicator of abuse and neglect. Governing bodies and proprietors should put in place appropriate safeguarding responses to children who go missing from education settings, particularly on repeat occasions, to help identify any risk of abuse and neglect including sexual abuse or exploitation and to help prevent the risks of their going missing in future.

---

[17] The Children and Families Act 2014 requires local authorities in England to appoint at least one person for the purpose of discharging the local authority's duty to promote the educational achievement of its looked after children. That person (known as the virtual school head) must be an officer employed by the authority or another local authority in England.

Part three: Safer recruitment

Recruitment, selection and pre-employment vetting

46.   It is vital that schools and colleges create a culture of safe recruitment and, as part of that, adopt recruitment procedures that help deter, reject or identify people who might abuse children. This part of the guidance describes in detail those checks that are, or may be, required for any individual working in any capacity at, or visiting, the school or college. Governing bodies and proprietors must act reasonably in making decisions about the suitability of the prospective employee based on checks and evidence including: criminal record checks (DBS checks), barred list checks and prohibition checks[18] together with references and interview information.

47.   The level of DBS check required, and whether a prohibition check is required, will depend on the role and duties of an applicant to work in a school or college, as outlined in this guidance.

48.   For most appointments, an enhanced DBS check with barred list information will be appropriate as the majority of staff will be engaging in regulated activity. A person will be considered to be in 'regulated activity' if as a result of their work they:

- will be responsible, on a regular basis, in any setting for the care or supervision of children; or

- will regularly work in a school or college at times when children are on school or college premises (where the person's work requires interaction with children, whether or not the work is paid (unless they are a supervised volunteer), or whether the person is directly employed or employed by a contractor); or

- in a college, will regularly come into contact with children under 18 years of age.

49.   In a school or college a **supervised** volunteer who regularly teaches or looks after children is not in regulated activity. The Department for Education (DfE) has published separate statutory guidance on supervision and regulated activity which schools and colleges should have regard to when considering which checks should be undertaken on volunteers. This is set out at Annex D.[19]

---

[18] Regulations 12 and 24 of the School Staffing (England) Regulations 2009, for maintained schools, applied to the management committee of pupil referral units through the Education (Pupil Referral Units) (Application of Enactment) (England) Regulations 2007. The Education (Independent School Standards) (England) Regulations 2010, Schedule 1, Part 4 apply to independent schools, including free schools and academies.

[19] 'Supervised' and 'unsupervised' have a particular meaning in relation to regulated activity.

Regulated activity

The full legal definition of regulated activity is set out in Schedule 4 of the Safeguarding Vulnerable Groups Act 2006 as amended by the Protection of Freedoms Act 2012. HM Government have produced a factual note on *Regulated Activity in relation to Children: scope.*

Regulated activity includes:

a) teaching, training, instructing, caring for (see (c) below) or supervising children if the person is unsupervised, or providing advice or guidance on well-being, or driving a vehicle only for children,

b) work for a limited range of establishments (known as 'specified places', which include schools and colleges), with the opportunity for contact with children, but not including work done by supervised volunteers;

Work under (a) or (b) is regulated activity only if done regularly.[20] Some activities are always regulated activities, regardless of their frequency or whether they are supervised or not. This includes:

c) relevant personal care, or health care provided by or provided under the supervision of a health care professional:

- personal care includes helping a child, for reasons of age, illness or disability, with eating or drinking, or in connection with toileting, washing, bathing and dressing;[21]

- health care means care for children provided by, or under the direction or supervision of, a regulated health care professional.

50.   In addition to the DBS checks described, anyone who is appointed to carry out teaching work will require an additional check to ensure they are not prohibited from teaching. See the pre-appointments section which follows.

---

[20] The Safeguarding Vulnerable Groups Act 2006 provides that the type of work referred to at (a) or (b) will be regulated activity if "it is carried out frequently by the same person" or if "the period condition is satisfied". Paragraph 10 of Schedule 4 to this Act says the period condition is satisfied if the person carrying out the activity does so at any time on more than three days in any period of 30 days and, for the purposes of the work referred to at (a), it is also satisfied if it is done at any time between 2am and 6am and it gives the person the opportunity to have face to face contact with children. "Frequently" is not defined in the Act, but the Guidance *Regulated Activity in relation to Children: scope* describes "frequently" as doing something once a week or more.

[21] It is not intended that personal care includes such activities as, for example, parent volunteers helping with costumes for school plays or helping a child lace up football boots.

Types of check

Disclosure and barring service (DBS checks)

51.   The DBS is responsible for administering three types of checks (see Annex E for more information):

- **Standard:** a check of the Police National Computer (PNC) records of convictions, cautions, reprimands and warnings;

- **Enhanced:** a check of the PNC records as above, plus other information held by the police that is considered relevant by the police; and

- **Enhanced with barred list information:** for people working in regulated activity with children. This adds checks of the DBS Children's Barred List to the enhanced check.[22]

More information is available on the DBS website.

52.   When the DBS has completed its check of an applicant's PNC record and, if appropriate, whether or not they are on the barred list, the relevant information will be recorded on a certificate (the DBS certificate) that is sent to the applicant. The applicant must show the DBS certificate to their potential employer before they take up post or as soon as practicable afterwards. If a school or college allows an individual to start work in regulated activity before the DBS certificate is available then they should ensure that the individual is appropriately supervised and that all other checks, including a separate barred list check, have been completed.

53.   **If a school or college knows or has reason to believe that an individual is barred, it commits an offence if it allows the individual to carry out any form of regulated activity.[23] There are penalties of up to five years in prison if a barred individual is convicted of attempting to engage or engaging in such work.[24]**

Secretary of State Prohibition Orders

54.   Prohibition orders prevent a person from carrying out teaching work in schools, sixth form colleges, 16 to 19 academies, relevant youth accommodation and children's homes in England.[25] A person who is prohibited from teaching must not be appointed to work as a teacher in such a setting. A check of any prohibition can be carried out using

---

[22] The DBS maintains 'barred lists' of individuals who are unsuitable for working with children and adults. The DBS lists replace the lists maintained by the former Independent Safeguarding Authority.

[23] Section 9, Safeguarding Vulnerable Groups Act 2006.

[24] Section 7, Safeguarding Vulnerable Groups Act 2006.

[25] Prohibition orders are made by the Secretary of State under section 141B of the Education Act 2002. Those made by the General Teaching Council for England (GTCE) prior to April 2012 have the same effect.

the Employer Access Online Service. [26] Prohibition orders are described in the National College for Teaching and Leadership's (NCTL) publication Teacher misconduct: the prohibition of teachers.

55.   Prohibition orders are made by the Secretary of State following consideration by a professional conduct panel convened by NCTL. Pending such consideration, the Secretary of State may issue an interim prohibition order if he considers that it is in the public interest to do so.

Pre-appointment checks

All new appointments to regulated activity

56.   An offer of appointment to a successful candidate, including one who has lived or worked abroad, must be conditional upon satisfactory completion of pre-employment checks.

57.   When appointing new staff, schools and colleges must:

- verify a candidate's identity, preferably from current photographic ID and proof of address except where, for exceptional reasons, none is available;

- obtain a certificate for an enhanced DBS check with a barred list information where the person will be engaging in regulated activity; [27]

- obtain a separate barred list check if an individual will start work in regulated activity before the DBS certificate is available;

- check that a candidate to be employed as a teacher is not subject to a prohibition order issued by the Secretary of State, using the Employer Access Online service;

- verify the candidate's mental and physical fitness to carry out their work responsibilities.[28] A job applicant can be asked relevant questions about disability and health in order to establish whether they have the physical and mental capacity for the specific role;[29]

---

[26] The Employer Access Online Service will also identify any existing prohibitions and sanctions made by the General Teaching Council for England (GTCE) before its abolition at the end of March 2012, and provide information about any teacher qualifications held and whether induction has been passed. The service is offered free of charge to schools, local authorities and teacher supply agencies in England.

[27] Regulations 17 and 24 of the School Staffing (England) Regulations 2009 for maintained schools also applied to the management committee of pupil referral units through the Education (Pupil Referral Units) (Application of Enactment) (England) Regulations 2007. The Education (Independent School Standards) (England) Regulations 2010, Schedule 1, Part 4 apply to independent schools, including free schools and academies.

[28] Education (Health Standards) (England) Regulations 2003 see also fitness to teach circular

[29] Section 60 of the Equality Act 2010.

- verify the person's right to work in the UK. If there is uncertainty about whether an individual needs permission to work in the UK, then prospective employers, or volunteer managers, should follow advice on the GOV.UK website;

- if the person has lived or worked outside the UK, make any further checks the school or college consider appropriate (see relevant sections below); and

- verify professional qualifications, as appropriate.

58. A DBS certificate must be obtained from the candidate before or as soon as practicable after appointment. Alternatively, if the applicant has subscribed to it and gives permission, the school or college may undertake an online update check through the DBS Update Service. Individuals can join the DBS Update Service when applying for a new DBS check; this will allow them to re-use this check when applying for similar jobs. With the individual's consent, their employer can go online and carry out a free, instant check to see if a new certificate is required: www.gov.uk/dbs-update-service.

59. There is **no requirement** to obtain an enhanced DBS check if, in the three months prior to beginning work in their new appointment, the applicant has worked:

- in a school in England in a post which brought them into regular contact with children or in any post in a school since 12 May 2006; or

- in a college in England in a position which involved the provision of education and regularly caring for, training, supervising or being in sole charge of children or young people under the age of 18.

But a school or college **may** request an enhanced DBS check with barred list information should there be concerns and bearing in mind the duty schools and colleges are under not to allow a barred person to work in regulated activity.

60. A school or college **may not** request an enhanced DBS check with barred list check for anyone working in the school or college who is not in regulated activity, but may request an enhanced DBS check **without** a barred list check.

Flowchart of Disclosure and Barring Service criminal record checks and barred list checks

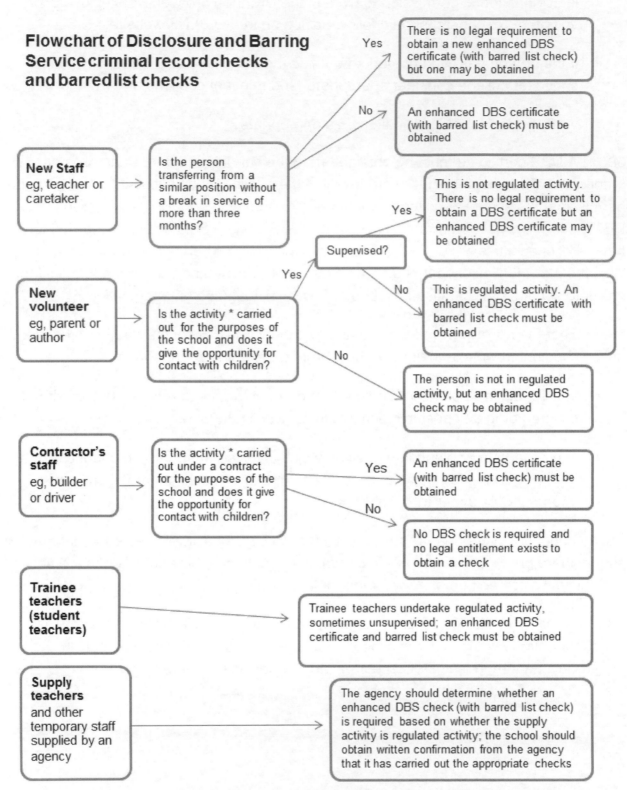

New Staff
eg, teacher or caretaker

Is the person transferring from a similar position without a break in service of more than three months?

Yes → There is no legal requirement to obtain a new enhanced DBS certificate (with barred list check) but one may be obtained

No → An enhanced DBS certificate (with barred list check) must be obtained

New volunteer
eg, parent or author

Is the activity * carried out for the purposes of the school and does it give the opportunity for contact with children?

Yes → Supervised?

Supervised? Yes → This is not regulated activity. There is no legal requirement to obtain a DBS certificate but an enhanced DBS certificate may be obtained

Supervised? No → This is regulated activity. An enhanced DBS certificate with barred list check must be obtained

No → The person is not in regulated activity, but an enhanced DBS check may be obtained

Contractor's staff
eg, builder or driver

Is the activity * carried out under a contract for the purposes of the school and does it give the opportunity for contact with children?

Yes → An enhanced DBS certificate (with barred list check) must be obtained

No → No DBS check is required and no legal entitlement exists to obtain a check

Trainee teachers (student teachers)

Trainee teachers undertake regulated activity, sometimes unsupervised; an enhanced DBS certificate and barred list check must be obtained

Supply teachers
and other temporary staff supplied by an agency

The agency should determine whether an enhanced DBS check (with barred list check) is required based on whether the supply activity is regulated activity; the school should obtain written confirmation from the agency that it has carried out the appropriate checks

* Activities listed under the guidance's definition of regulated activity and which are carried out 'frequently'

Employment history and references

61.   Employers should always ask for written information about previous employment history and check that information is not contradictory or incomplete. If a candidate for a teaching post is not currently employed as a teacher, it is also advisable to check with the school, college or local authority at which they were most recently employed, to confirm details of their employment and their reasons for leaving.

62.   The purpose of seeking references is to obtain objective and factual information to support appointment decisions. References should always be obtained, scrutinised and any concerns resolved satisfactorily, before the appointment is confirmed. They should always be requested directly from the referee and employers should not rely on open references, for example in the form of 'to whom it may concern' testimonials.

63.   Ideally, references should be sought on all short-listed candidates, including internal ones, before interview, so that any issues of concern they raise can be explored further with the referee, and taken up with the candidate at interview.

64.   On receipt, references should be checked to ensure that all specific questions have been answered satisfactorily. The referee should be contacted to provide further clarification as appropriate: for example if the answers are vague. They should also be compared for consistency with the information provided by the candidate on their application form. Any discrepancies should be taken up with the candidate.

65.   Any information about past disciplinary action or allegations should be considered carefully when assessing the applicant's suitability for the post (including information obtained from the Employer Access Online checks referred to previously).

Single central record

66.   Schools and colleges must keep a single central record, referred to in the regulations (described in the following paragraph) as the register. The single central record must cover the following people:

- all staff (including supply staff) who work at the school: in colleges, this means those providing education to children;

- all others who work in regular contact with children in the school or college, including volunteers; and

- for independent schools, including academies and free schools, all members of the proprietor body.

Generally, the information to be recorded on these individuals is whether or not the following checks have been carried out or certificates obtained, and the date on which the checks were completed:

- an identity check;

- a barred list check;

- an enhanced DBS check;

- a prohibition from teaching check;

- further checks on people living or working outside the UK;

- a check of professional qualifications; and

- a check to establish the person's right to work in the United Kingdom.

67.   For details of records that must be kept, see:

- for maintained schools: Schedule 2 to the School Staffing (England) Regulations 2009 and the School Staffing (England) Amendment Regulations 2013 for pupil referral units through the Education (Pupil Referral Units) (Application of Enactment) (England) Regulations 2007

- for independent schools, (including academies and free schools and alternative provision academies and free schools): under the Education (Independent School Standards) (England) Regulations 2010, as amended by the Education (Independent School Standards) (England) (Amendment) Regulations 2012

- for colleges: the Further Education (Providers of Education) (England) regulations 2006 [30]

Schools and colleges do not have to keep copies of DBS certificates in order to fulfil the duty of maintaining the single central record. To help schools and colleges comply with the requirements of the Data Protection Act, where a school or college chooses to retain a copy they should not be retained for longer than six months. A copy of the other documents used to verify the successful candidate's identity, right to work and required qualifications should be kept for the personnel file.

Individuals who have lived or worked outside the UK

68.   Individuals who have lived or worked outside the UK must undergo the same checks as all other staff in schools or colleges. In addition, schools and colleges must make any further checks they think appropriate so that any relevant events that occurred outside the UK can be considered.

69.   Advice on the criminal record information which may be obtained from overseas police forces, published by the Home Office, is on GOV.UK. The Department for Education has also issued guidance on the employment of overseas-trained teachers This gives information on the requirements for overseas-trained teachers from the

---

[30] 16-19 academies and free schools are covered through their funding agreements.

European Economic Area to teach in England, and the award of qualified teacher status for teachers qualified in Australia, Canada, New Zealand and the United States of America.

Agency and third-party staff

70.   Schools and colleges must obtain written notification from any agency, or third-party organisation, they use that the organisation has carried out the checks on an individual who will be working at the school or college that the school or college would otherwise perform. This must include, as necessary, a barred list check, prior to appointing that individual. They must also check that the person presenting themselves for work is the same person on whom the checks have been made.

Trainee/student teachers

71.   Where applicants for initial teacher training are salaried by the school or college, the school or college must ensure that all necessary checks are carried out. As trainee teachers can undertake regulated activity, sometimes unsupervised, an enhanced DBS certificate and barred list check must be obtained. Where trainee teachers are fee-funded it is the responsibility of the initial teacher training provider to carry out the necessary checks.[31]

Existing staff

72.   If a school or college has concerns about an existing staff member's suitability to work with children, the school or college should carry out all relevant checks as if the person were a new member of staff. Similarly, if a person working at the school or college moves from a post that was not regulated activity, into work which is regulated activity, the relevant checks for the regulated activity must be carried out.[32] Apart from these circumstances, the school or college is not required to request a DBS check or barred list check.

73.   **Schools and colleges have a legal duty to refer to the DBS anyone who has harmed, or poses a risk of harm, to a child, or if there is reason to believe the member of staff has committed one of a number of listed offences, and who has been removed from working (paid or unpaid) in regulated activity, or would have**

---

[31] National College for Teaching and Leadership - Initial teacher training provider supporting advice and initial teacher training criteria

[32] Schools will wish to consider the offence of allowing individuals to engage in regulated activity whilst barred. It is intended that, at a date to be announced, schools (as a regulated activity provider) will be under a duty to request a barred list check before allowing any individuals to engage in regulated activity (section 34ZA Safeguarding Vulnerable Groups Act 2006) and for it to be possible to obtain such a check independently from the enhanced check from the DBS.

been removed had they not left.[33] The DBS will consider whether to bar the person. Referrals should be made as soon as possible after the resignation or removal of the individual.

74.   Where a teacher's employer, including an agency, ceases to use the services of a teacher because of serious misconduct, or would have dismissed them had they not left first, they must consider whether to refer the case to the Secretary of State, as required by sections 141D and 141E of the Education Act 2002. The Secretary of State may investigate the case, and if s/he finds there is a case to answer, must then decide whether to make a prohibition order in respect of the person.

Volunteers

75.   Under no circumstances should a volunteer in respect of whom no checks have been obtained be left unsupervised or allowed to work in regulated activity.

76.   For new volunteers in regulated activity who will regularly teach or look after children on an unsupervised basis or provide personal care on a one-off basis schools and colleges must obtain an enhanced DBS certificate with barred list check.[34]

77.   For new volunteers not in regulated activity schools and colleges should obtain an enhanced DBS certificate.

78.   For existing volunteers who provide personal care, the school or college should consider obtaining an enhanced DBS certificate with barred list check.

79.   For other existing volunteers who are unsupervised and continuing with their current duties, unless there is cause for concern the school or college should not request a DBS check with barred list check because the volunteer should already have been checked.

80.   For existing volunteers not in regulated activity there is **no requirement** to request an enhanced DBS check. However the school or college may choose to request one as they judge necessary but **may not** request a check of the barred list.

81.   If a volunteer is not engaging in regulated activity, the school or college should undertake a risk assessment and use their professional judgement and experience when deciding whether to seek an enhanced DBS check. They should consider:

- the nature of the work with children;

---

[33] The list of offences is set out in the Safeguarding Vulnerable Groups Act 2006 (Prescribed Criteria and Miscellaneous Provisions) Regulations 2009 (SI 2009 No. 37) (amended).

[34] At a future date to be announced, all organisations will have a duty to obtain a barred list check on a volunteer who will be engaging in regulated activity.

- what the establishment knows about the volunteer, including formal or informal information offered by staff, parents and other volunteers;

- whether the volunteer has other employment or undertakes voluntary activities where referees can advise on suitability; and

- whether the role is eligible for an enhanced DBS check.

82.   The Protection of Freedoms Act 2012 amended the Safeguarding Vulnerable Groups Act 2006, removing supervised volunteers from regulated activity and applying a duty on the Secretary of State to issue guidance to assist regulated activity providers such as schools and colleges, to decide what level of supervision is required so that this exclusion would apply. If the volunteer is to be supervised while undertaking an activity which would be regulated activity if it was unsupervised, the statutory guidance must be followed. This is replicated at Annex D. The guidance issued following this change requires that:

- there must be supervision by a person who is in regulated activity;[35]

- the supervision must be regular and day to day; and

- the supervision must be "reasonable in all the circumstances to ensure the protection of children".

83.   Employers are not legally allowed to request a barred list check on a volunteer who, because they are supervised, is not in regulated activity.

School and college governors

84.   School and college governors who are volunteers should be treated on the same basis as other volunteers, that is, an enhanced DBS check with barred list check should only be requested if the governor will be engaged in regulated activity. Governing bodies and proprietors can request an enhanced DBS check without a barred list check on an individual as part of the appointment process for governors.

Contractors

85.   Schools and colleges should have arrangements in place with contractors to make sure that the contractor, or any employee of the contractor, working at the school or college has been subject to the appropriate level of DBS check, if any such check is required (for example because the contractor is carrying out teaching or providing some type of care for or supervision of children regularly).

---

[35] If the work is in a specified place such as a school, paid workers remain in regulated activity even if supervised.

86.   Contractors and contractors' employees for whom an appropriate DBS check has not been undertaken should be supervised if they will have contact with children.

87.   If a contractor working at a school or college is self-employed, the school or college should consider obtaining the DBS check, as self-employed people are not able to make an application directly to the DBS on their own account.

88.   Schools and colleges should always check the identity of contractors and their staff on arrival at the school or college.

Visitors

89.   Schools and colleges do not have the power to request DBS checks and barred list checks, or ask to see DBS certificates, for visitors (for example children's' relatives or other visitors attending a sports day). Headteachers and principals should use their professional judgment about the need to escort or supervise visitors.

Adults who supervise children on work experience

90.   Schools and colleges organising work experience placements should ensure that policies and procedures are in place to protect children from harm.

91.   Barred list checks by the DBS might be required on some people who supervise a child under the age of 16 on a work experience placement.[36] The school or college would have to consider the specific circumstances of the work experience, in particular the nature of the supervision and the frequency of the activity being supervised, to determine what, if any, checks are necessary. These considerations would include whether the person providing the teaching/training/instruction/supervision to the child will be:

- unsupervised; and

- providing the teaching/training/instruction frequently (at least once a week or on more than three days in a 30 day period, or overnight).

92.   If the person working with the child is unsupervised and the same person is in frequent contact with the child, the work is likely to be regulated activity. If so, the school or college could ask the employer providing the work experience to ensure that the person providing the instruction or training is not a barred person.

93.   Schools and colleges are not able to request an enhanced DBS check with barred list information for staff supervising children aged 16 to 17 on work experience.[37]

---

[36] Safeguarding Vulnerable Groups Act 2006, as amended by the Protection of Freedoms Act 2012, which came into force on 10 September 2012.
[37] The Rehabilitation of Offenders Act 1974 (Exceptions) Order 1975 was amended by the Rehabilitation of Offenders Act 1974 (Exceptions) (Amendment) (England and Wales) Order 2012 so that employers may no longer request checks in these circumstances.

94.   If the activity undertaken by the child on work experience takes place in a 'specified place', such as a school or college, and gives the opportunity for contact with children, this may itself be considered to be regulated activity. In these cases and where the child is 16 years of age or over, the work experience provider should consider whether a DBS enhanced check should be requested for the child/young person in question. DBS checks cannot be requested for children/young people under the age of 16.[38]

Proprietors of independent schools including academies and free schools or alternative provision academies and free schools[39]

95.   Before an individual becomes either the proprietor of an independent school or the chair of a body of people which is the proprietor of an independent school[40], the Secretary of State will:[41]

- carry out an enhanced DBS check;

- confirm the individual's identity; and

- if the individual lives or has lived outside of the UK, making an enhanced check insufficient, such other checks as the Secretary of State considers appropriate.

96.   The Secretary of State also undertakes these checks in respect of the chair of governing bodies of a non-maintained special school.[42]

97.   The requirement for an enhanced DBS check is disapplied for the chair of an academy trust if the academy is converting from a maintained school and the person has already been subject to a check carried out by the local authority.[43]

98.   Where the proprietor is a body of people, the chair must ensure that enhanced DBS certificates are obtained for the other members of the body and that identity checks are completed before, or as soon as practicable after, any individual takes up their position. Further checks as the chair considers appropriate should be undertaken where, by reason of the individual's living or having lived overseas, obtaining an enhanced DBS check is not sufficient to establish his or her suitability to work in a school.

---

[38] Under the Police Act 1997, an individual must be 16 or over to be able to make an application for a DBS check.

[39] The proprietor of an academy or free school or alternative provision academy or free school is the academy trust.

[40] This will include an academy trust of any academy or free school, other than for 16 – 19 academies or free schools.

[41] Education (Independent School Standards) (England) Regulations 2010, Schedule 1, Part 4.

[42] Education (Non-Maintained Special Schools) (England) Regulations 2011, Para 4 of Schedule 1.

[43] Paragraph (7), standard 21, Education (Independent School Standards) (England) Regulations 2010.

99.   In the case of an academy trust newly established to operate a free school, the DfE will ask the DBS to conduct checks on all members and directors of the new trust. Academy trusts, including those established to run a free school, have the same responsibilities as all independent schools in relation to requesting enhanced DBS certificates for permanent and supply staff.[44]

Children staying with host families

100.   Schools and colleges quite often make arrangements for their children to have learning experiences where, for short periods, the children may be provided with care and accommodation by a host family to which they are not related. This might happen, for example, but not only, as part of a foreign exchange visit or sports tour. Such arrangements could amount to "private fostering" under the Children Act 1989 or the Safeguarding Vulnerable Groups Act 2006, or both. See Annex C for further details.

---

[44] The Education (Independent School Standards) (England) Regulations 2010, Schedule 1, Part 4. The regulation does not apply to 16-19 free school academies.

Part four: Allegations of abuse made against teachers and other staff

Duties as an employer and an employee

101.   This part of the guidance is about managing cases of allegations that might indicate a person would pose a risk of harm if they continue to work in regular or close contact with children in their present position, or in any capacity. It should be used in respect of all cases in which it is alleged that a teacher or member of staff (including volunteers) in a school or college that provides education for children under 18 years of age has:

- behaved in a way that has harmed a child, or may have harmed a child;
- possibly committed a criminal offence against or related to a child; or
- behaved towards a child or children in a way that indicates he or she would pose a risk of harm if they work regularly or closely with children.

102.   This part of the guidance relates to members of staff who are currently working in any school or colllege regardless of whether the school or college is where the alleged abuse took place. Allegations against a teacher who is no longer teaching should be referred to the police.

103.   Employers have a duty of care to their employees. They should ensure they provide effective support for anyone facing an allegation and provide the employee with a named contact if they are suspended. It is essential that any allegation of abuse made against a teacher or other member of staff or volunteer in a school or college is dealt with very quickly, in a fair and consistent way that provides effective protection for the child and at the same time supports the person who is the subject of the allegation.

Initial considerations

104.   The procedures for dealing with allegations need to be applied with common sense and judgement. Many cases may well either not meet the criteria set out above, or may do so without warranting consideration of either a police investigation or enquiries by local authority children's social care services. In these cases, local arrangements should be followed to resolve cases without delay.

105.   Some rare allegations will be so serious they require immediate intervention by children's social care services and/or police. The Local Authority Designated Officer (LADO) should be informed of all allegations that come to a school or college's attention and appear to meet the criteria so they can consult police and children's social care services as appropriate.

106. The following definitions should be used when determining the outcome of allegation investigations:

- **Substantiated:** there is sufficient evidence to prove the allegation;

- **Malicious**: there is sufficient evidence to disprove the allegation and there has been a deliberate act to deceive;

- **False:** there is sufficient evidence to disprove the allegation;

- **Unsubstantiated**: there is insufficient evidence to either to prove or disprove the allegation. The term, therefore, does not imply guilt or innocence.

107. In the first instance, the head teacher or principal, or chair of governors, chair of the management committee or proprietor of an independent school (the 'case manager') should immediately discuss the allegation with the LADO. The purpose of an initial discussion is for the LADO and the case manager to consider the nature, content and context of the allegation and agree a course of action. The LADO may ask the case manager to provide or obtain relevant additional information, such as previous history, whether the child or their family have made similar allegations previously and the individual's current contact with children. There may be situations when the case manager will want to involve the police immediately, for example if the person is deemed to be an immediate risk to children or there is evidence of a possible criminal offence. Where there is no such evidence, the case manager should discuss the allegations with the LADO in order to help determine whether police involvement is necessary.

108. The initial sharing of information and evaluation may lead to a decision that no further action is to be taken in regard to the individual facing the allegation or concern; in which case this decision and a justification for it should be recorded by both the case manager and the LADO, and agreement reached on what information should be put in writing to the individual concerned and by whom. The case manager should then consider with the LADO what action should follow both in respect of the individual and those who made the initial allegation.

109. The case manager should inform the accused person about the allegation as soon as possible after consulting the LADO. It is extremely important that the case manager provides them with as much information as possible at that time. However, where a strategy discussion is needed, or police or children's social care services need to be involved, the case manager should not do that until those agencies have been consulted, and have agreed what information can be disclosed to the accused. Employers must consider carefully whether the circumstances of a case warrant a person being suspended from contact with children at the school or college or whether alternative arrangements can be put in place until the allegation or concern is resolved. All options to avoid suspension should be considered prior to taking that step (see further information on suspension which follows).

110.   If there is cause to suspect a child is suffering or is likely to suffer significant harm, a strategy discussion should be convened in accordance with *Working Together to Safeguard Children*. If the allegation is about physical contact, the strategy discussion or initial evaluation with the police should take into account that teachers and other school and college staff are entitled to use reasonable force to control or restrain children in certain circumstances, including dealing with disruptive behaviour.

111.   Where it is clear that an investigation by the police or children's social care services is unnecessary, or the strategy discussion or initial evaluation decides that is the case, the LADO should discuss the next steps with the case manager. In those circumstances, the options open to the school or college depend on the nature and circumstances of the allegation and the evidence and information available. This will range from taking no further action to dismissal or a decision not to use the person's services in future. Suspension should not be the default position: an individual should be suspended only if there is no reasonable alternative.

112.   In some cases, further enquiries will be needed to enable a decision about how to proceed. If so, the LADO should discuss with the case manager how and by whom the investigation will be undertaken. In straightforward cases, the investigation should normally be undertaken by a senior member of the school or college's staff.

113.   However, in other circumstances, such as lack of appropriate resource within the school or college, or the nature or complexity of the allegation will require an independent investigator. Many local authorities already provide for an independent investigation of allegations, often as part of the personnel services that maintained schools and colleges can buy in from the authority. It is important that local authorities ensure that schools and colleges have access to an affordable facility for independent investigation where that is appropriate.

Supporting those involved

114.   Employers have a duty of care to their employees. They should act to manage and minimise the stress inherent in the allegations process. Support for the individual is vital to fulfilling this duty. Individuals should be informed of concerns or allegations as soon as possible and given an explanation of the likely course of action, unless there is an objection by the children's social care services or the police. The individual should be advised to contact their trade union representative, if they have one, or a colleague for support. They should also be given access to welfare counselling or medical advice where this is provided by the employer.

115.   The case manager should appoint a named representative to keep the person who is the subject of the allegation informed of the progress of the case and consider what other support is appropriate for the individual. For staff in maintained schools and colleges, that may include support via the local authority occupational health or employee welfare arrangements. Particular care needs to be taken when employees are

suspended to ensure that they are kept informed of both the progress of their case and current work-related issues. Social contact with colleagues and friends should not be prevented unless there is evidence to suggest that such contact is likely to be prejudicial to the gathering and presentation of evidence.

116.   Parents or carers of a child or children involved should be told about the allegation as soon as possible if they do not already know of it. However, where a strategy discussion is required, or police or children's social care services need to be involved, the case manager should not do so until those agencies have been consulted and have agreed what information can be disclosed to the parents or carers. Parents or carers should also be kept informed about the progress of the case, and told the outcome where there is not a criminal prosecution, including the outcome of any disciplinary process. The deliberations of a disciplinary hearing, and the information taken into account in reaching a decision, cannot normally be disclosed, but the parents or carers of the child should be told the outcome in confidence.[45]

117.   Parents and carers should also be made aware of the prohibition on reporting or publishing allegations about teachers in section 141F of the Education Act 2002 (see below). If parents or carers wish to apply to the court to have reporting restrictions removed, they should be told to seek legal advice.

118.   In cases where a child may have suffered significant harm, or there may be a criminal prosecution, children's social care services, or the police as appropriate, should consider what support the child or children involved may need.

Confidentiality

119.   It is extremely important that when an allegation is made, the school or college makes every effort to maintain confidentiality and guard against unwanted publicity while an allegation is being investigated or considered. The Education Act 2011 introduced reporting restrictions preventing the publication of any material that may lead to the identification of a teacher who has been accused by, or on behalf of, a pupil from the same school or college (where that identification would identify the teacher as the subject of the allegation). The reporting restrictions apply until the point that the accused person is charged with an offence, or until the Secretary of State[46] or the General Teaching Council for Wales publishes information about an investigation or decision in a disciplinary case arising from the allegation. The reporting restrictions also cease to apply if the individual to whom the restrictions apply effectively waives their right to anonymity by going public themselves or by giving their written consent for another to do so or if a judge lifts restrictions in response to a request to do so. The provisions commenced on 1 October 2012.

---

[45] In deciding what information to disclose, careful consideration should be given to the provisions of the Data Protection Act 1998, the law of confidence and, where relevant, the Human Rights Act 1998.
[46] Carried out by the National College for Teaching and Leadership.

120. The legislation imposing restrictions makes clear that "publication" of material that may lead to the identification of the teacher who is the subject of the allegation is prohibited. "Publication" includes "any speech, writing, relevant programme or other communication in whatever form, which is addressed to the public at large or any section of the public". This means that a parent who, for example, published details of the allegation on a social networking site would be in breach of the reporting restrictions (if what was published could lead to the identification of the teacher by members of the public).

121. In accordance with the Association of Chief Police Officers' (ACPO) guidance the police will not normally provide any information to the press or media that might identify an individual who is under investigation, unless and until the person is charged with a criminal offence. (In exceptional cases where the police would like to depart from that rule, for example an appeal to trace a suspect, they must apply to a magistrates' court to request that reporting restrictions be lifted).

122. The case manager should take advice from the LADO, police and children's social care services to agree the following:

- who needs to know and, importantly, exactly what information can be shared;

- how to manage speculation, leaks and gossip;

- what, if any information can be reasonably given to the wider community to reduce speculation; and

- how to manage press interest if and when it should arise.

Managing the situation and exit arrangements

Resignations and 'settlement/compromise agreements'

123. If the accused person resigns, or ceases to provide their services, this should not prevent an allegation being followed up in accordance with this guidance. **A referral to the DBS *must* be made, if the criteria are met – see paragraph 73**. If the accused person resigns or their services cease to be used and the criteria are met it will not be appropriate to reach a settlement/compromise agreement. A settlement/compromise agreement which prevents the school or college from making a DBS referral when the criteria are met would likely result in a criminal offence being committed as the school or college would not be complying with its legal duty to make the referral.

124. It is important that every effort is made to reach a conclusion in all cases of allegations bearing on the safety or welfare of children, including any in which the person concerned refuses to cooperate with the process. Wherever possible the accused should be given a full opportunity to answer the allegation and make representations about it.

But the process of recording the allegation and any supporting evidence, and reaching a judgement about whether it can be substantiated on the basis of all the information available, should continue even if that cannot be done or the accused does not cooperate. It may be difficult to reach a conclusion in those circumstances, and it may not be possible to apply any disciplinary sanctions if a person's period of notice expires before the process is complete, but it is important to reach and record a conclusion wherever possible.

125.   So-called 'settlement/compromise agreements', by which a person agrees to resign if the employer agrees not to pursue disciplinary action, and both parties agree a form of words to be used in any future reference, should not be used in cases of refusal to cooperate or resignation before the person's notice period expires. Such an agreement will not prevent a thorough police investigation where that is appropriate.

Record keeping

126.   Details of allegations that are found to have been malicious should be removed from personnel records. However, for all other allegations, it is important that a clear and comprehensive summary of the allegation, details of how the allegation was followed up and resolved, and a note of any action taken and decisions reached, is kept on the confidential personnel file of the accused, and a copy provided to the person concerned.

127.   The purpose of the record is to enable accurate information to be given in response to any future request for a reference, where appropriate. It will provide clarification in cases where future DBS checks reveal information from the police about an allegation that did not result in a criminal conviction and it will help to prevent unnecessary re-investigation if, as sometimes happens, an allegation re-surfaces after a period of time. The record should be retained at least until the accused has reached normal retirement age or for a period of 10 years from the date of the allegation if that is longer.

128.   The Information Commissioner has published guidance on employment records in its Employment Practices Code and supplementary guidance, which provides some practical advice on employment retention.[47]

References

129.   Cases in which an allegation was proven to be false, unsubstantiated or malicious should not be included in employer references. A history of repeated concerns or allegations which have all been found to be false, unsubstantiated or malicious should also not be included in any reference.

---

[47] Information Commissioners Office – Guidance on employment records in its Employment Practices Code and supplementary guidance

Timescales

130.   It is in everyone's interest to resolve cases as quickly as possible consistent with a fair and thorough investigation. All allegations should be investigated as a priority to avoid any delay. Target timescales are shown below: the time taken to investigate and resolve individual cases depends on a variety of factors including the nature, seriousness and complexity of the allegation, but these targets should be achieved in all but truly exceptional cases. It is expected that 80 per cent of cases should be resolved within one month, 90 per cent within three months, and all but the most exceptional cases should be completed within 12 months.

131.   For those cases where it is clear immediately that the allegation is unsubstantiated or malicious, they should be resolved within one week. Where the initial consideration decides that the allegation does not involve a possible criminal offence it will be for the employer to deal with it, although if there are concerns about child protection, the employer should discuss them with the LADO. In such cases, if the nature of the allegation does not require formal disciplinary action, the employer should institute appropriate action within three working days. If a disciplinary hearing is required and can be held without further investigation, the hearing should be held within 15 working days.

Oversight and monitoring

132.   The LADO has overall responsibility for oversight of the procedures for dealing with allegations; for resolving any inter-agency issues; and for liaison with the Local Safeguarding Children Board (LSCB) on the subject. The LADO will provide advice and guidance to the case manager, in addition to liaising with the police and other agencies, and monitoring the progress of cases to ensure that they are dealt with as quickly as possible consistent with a thorough and fair process. Reviews should be conducted at fortnightly or monthly intervals, depending on the complexity of the case.

133.   Police forces should also identify officers who will be responsible for:

- liaising with the LADO;

- taking part in the strategy discussion or initial evaluation;

- subsequently reviewing the progress of those cases in which there is a police investigation; and

- sharing information on completion of the investigation or any prosecution.

134.   If the strategy discussion or initial assessment decides that a police investigation is required, the police should also set a target date for reviewing the progress of the investigation and consulting the Crown Prosecution Service (CPS) about whether to: charge the individual; continue to investigate; or close the investigation. Wherever possible, that review should take place no later than four weeks after the initial

evaluation. Dates for subsequent reviews, ideally at fortnightly intervals, should be set at the meeting if the investigation continues.

Suspension

135.   The possible risk of harm to children posed by an accused person should be evaluated and managed in respect of the child(ren) involved in the allegations. In some rare cases that will require the case manager to consider suspending the accused until the case is resolved. Suspension should not be an automatic response when an allegation is reported; all options to avoid suspension should be considered prior to taking that step. If the case manager is concerned about the welfare of other children in the community or the teacher's family, those concerns should be reported to the LADO or police. But suspension is highly unlikely to be justified on the basis of such concerns alone.

136.   Suspension should be considered only in a case where there is cause to suspect a child or other children at the school or college is/are at risk of harm or the case is so serious that it might be grounds for dismissal. However, a person should not be suspended automatically: the case manager must consider carefully whether the circumstances warrant suspension from contact with children at the school or college or until the allegation is resolved, and may wish to seek advice from their personnel adviser and the LADO. In cases where the school or college is made aware that the Secretary of State has made an interim prohibition order in respect of an individual at the school or college it will be necessary to immediately suspend that person from teaching pending the findings of the NCTL's investigation.

137.   The case manager should also consider whether the result that would be achieved by immediate suspension could be obtained by alternative arrangements. In many cases an investigation can be resolved quickly and without the need for suspension. If the LADO, police and children's social care services have no objections to the member of staff continuing to work during the investigation, the case manager should be as inventive as possible to avoid suspension. Based on assessment of risk, the following alternatives should be considered by the case manager before suspending a member of staff:

- redeployment within the school or college so that the individual does not have direct contact with the child or children concerned;

- providing an assistant to be present when the individual has contact with children;

- redeploying to alternative work in the school or college so the individual does not have unsupervised access to children;

- moving the child or children to classes where they will not come into contact with the member of staff, making it clear that this is not a punishment and parents have been consulted; or

- temporarily redeploying the member of staff to another role in a different location, for example to an alternative school or college or work for the local authority or academy trust.

138.   These alternatives allow time for an informed decision regarding the suspension and possibly reduce the initial impact of the allegation. This will, however, depend upon the nature of the allegation. The case manager should consider the potential permanent professional reputational damage to employees that can result from suspension where an allegation is later found to be unsubstantiated or maliciously intended.

139.   If immediate suspension is considered necessary, the rationale and justification for such a course of action should be agreed and recorded by both the case manager and the LADO. This should also include what alternatives to suspension have been considered and why they were rejected.

140.   Where it has been deemed appropriate to suspend the person, written confirmation should be dispatched within one working day, giving as much detail as appropriate for the reasons for the suspension. It is not acceptable for an employer to leave a person who has been suspended without any support. The person should be informed at the point of their suspension who their named contact is within the organisation and provided with their contact details.

141.   Children's social care services or the police cannot require the case manager to suspend a member of staff or a volunteer, although they should give appropriate weight to their advice. The power to suspend is vested in the proprietor of the school, or governing bodies of the school or college who are the employers of staff at the school or college. However, where a strategy discussion or initial evaluation concludes that there should be enquiries by the children's social care services and/or an investigation by the police, the LADO should canvass police and children's social care services for views about whether the accused member of staff needs to be suspended from contact with children in order to inform the school or college consideration of suspension. Police involvement does not make it mandatory to suspend a member of staff; this decision should be taken on a case-by-case basis having undertaken a risk assessment.

Information sharing

142.   In a strategy discussion or the initial evaluation of the case, the agencies involved should share all relevant information they have about the person who is the subject of the allegation, and about the alleged victim.

143.   Where the police are involved, wherever possible the employer should ask the police to obtain consent from the individuals involved to share their statements and evidence for use in the employer disciplinary process. This should be done as their investigation proceeds and will enable the police to share relevant information without delay at the conclusion of their investigation or any court case.

144.   Children's social care services should adopt a similar procedure when making enquiries to determine whether the child or children named in the allegation are in need of protection or services, so that any information obtained in the course of those enquiries which is relevant to a disciplinary case can be passed to the employer without delay.

Specific actions

Following a criminal investigation or a prosecution

145.   The police should inform the employer and LADO immediately when a criminal investigation and any subsequent trial is complete, or if it is decided to close an investigation without charge, or not to continue to prosecute the case after person has been charged. In those circumstances the LADO should discuss with the case manager whether any further action, including disciplinary action, is appropriate and, if so, how to proceed. The information provided by the police and/or children's social care services should inform that decision. The options will depend on the circumstances of the case and the consideration will need to take into account the result of the police investigation or the trial, as well as the different standard of proof required in disciplinary and criminal proceedings.

On conclusion of a case

146.   If the allegation is substantiated and the person is dismissed or the employer ceases to use the person's services, or the person resigns or otherwise ceases to provide his or her services, the LADO should discuss with the case manager and their personnel adviser whether the school or college will decide to make a referral to the DBS for consideration of inclusion on the barred lists is required;[48] and in the case of a member of teaching staff whether to refer the matter to the National College for Teaching and Leadership (NCTL) to consider prohibiting the individual from teaching.

147.   **There is a legal requirement for employers to make a referral to the DBS where they think that an individual has engaged in conduct that harmed (or is likely to harm) a child; or if a person otherwise poses a risk of harm to a child. See paragraph 73.**

148.   Where it is decided on the conclusion of a case that a person who has been suspended can return to work, the case manager should consider how best to facilitate that. Most people will benefit from some help and support to return to work after a stressful experience. Depending on the individual's circumstances, a phased return and/or the provision of a mentor to provide assistance and support in the short term may be appropriate. The case manager should also consider how the person's contact with

---

[48] Disclosure and Barring Service – guidance on Referrals to the DBS

the child or children who made the allegation can best be managed if they are still a pupil at the school or college.

In respect of malicious or unsubstantiated allegations

149.　If an allegation is determined to be unsubstantiated or malicious, the LADO should refer the matter to the children's social care services to determine whether the child concerned is in need of services, or may have been abused by someone else. If an allegation is shown to be deliberately invented or malicious, the headteacher, principal or proprietor should consider whether any disciplinary action is appropriate against the pupil who made it; or whether the police should be asked to consider if action might be appropriate against the person responsible, even if he or she was not a pupil.

Learning lessons

150.　At the conclusion of a case in which an allegation *is* substantiated, the LADO should review the circumstances of the case with the case manager to determine whether there are any improvements to be made to the school or college's procedures or practice to help prevent similar events in the future. This should include issues arising from the decision to suspend the member of staff, the duration of the suspension and whether or not suspension was justified. Lessons should also be learnt from the use of suspension when the individual is subsequently reinstated. The LADO and case manager should consider how future investigations of a similar nature could be carried out without suspending the individual.

Further information

151.　See the Crown Prosecution Service published guidance for the police under the Protection from Harassment Act 1997.

Annex A: Legislation

This guidance refers to the legislation below:

Education

- The Children Act 1989 and 2004

- Education Act 2002

- The Education (Health Standards) (England) Regulations 2003

- The Further Education (Providers of Education) (England) (Regulations) 2006

- The Education (Pupil Referral Units) (Application of Enactment) (England) Regulations 2007 as amended by SI 2010/1919, SI 2012/ 1201, SI 2012/1825, SI 2012/3158

- The School Staffing (England) Regulations 2009 as amended by SI 2012/1740 and SI 2013/1940

- The Education (Independent School Standards) (England) Regulations 2010 as amended by SI 2012/2962

- The Education (Non-Maintained Special Schools) (England) Regulations 2011

Police

- Police Act 1997

- The Police Act 1997 (Criminal Records) Regulations 2002, as amended

- The Police Act 1997 (Criminal Records) (No 2) Regulations 2009, as amended

Other

- Safeguarding Vulnerable Groups Act 2006

- Protection of Freedoms Act 2012

- Equality Act 2010

- The Common Law Duty of Care

- The Rehabilitation of Offenders Act 1974 (Exceptions) Order 1975, as amended

Annex B: Role of the designated safeguarding lead

Governing bodies and proprietors should ensure that the school or college designates an appropriate senior member of staff to take lead responsibility for child protection. This person should have the status and authority within the school to carry out the duties of the post including committing resources and, where appropriate, supporting and directing other staff.

The broad areas of responsibility for the designated safeguarding lead are:

Managing referrals

- Refer all cases of suspected abuse to the local authority children's social care and:

    - The local authority designated officer (LADO) for child protection concerns (all cases which concern a staff member);

    - Disclosure and Barring Service (cases where a person is dismissed or left due to risk/harm to a child); and/or

    - Police (cases where a crime may have been committed).

- Liaise with the headteacher or principal to inform him or her of issues especially ongoing enquiries under section 47 of the Children Act 1989 and police investigations

- Act as a source of support, advice and expertise to staff on matters of safety and safeguarding and when deciding whether to make a referral by liaising with relevant agencies

Training

- The designated safeguarding lead should receive appropriate training carried out every two years in order to:

    - Understand the assessment process for providing early help and intervention, for example through locally agreed common and shared assessment processes such as early help assessments

    - Have a working knowledge of how local authorities conduct a child protection case conference and a child protection review conference and be able to attend and contribute to these effectively when required to do so

    - Ensure each member of staff has access to and understands the school's or college's child protection policy and procedures, especially new and part time staff

- Be alert to the specific needs of children in need,[49] those with special educational needs and young carers

- Be able to keep detailed, accurate, secure written records of concerns and referrals

- Obtain access to resources and attend any relevant or refresher training courses

- Encourage a culture of listening to children and taking account of their wishes and feelings, among all staff, in any measures the school or college may put in place to protect them

Raising Awareness

- The designated safeguarding lead should ensure the school or college's policies are known and used appropriately:

  - Ensure the school or college's child protection policy is reviewed annually and the procedures and implementation are updated and reviewed regularly, and work with governing bodies or proprietors regarding this

  - Ensure the child protection policy is available publicly and parents are aware of the fact that referrals about suspected abuse or neglect may be made and the role of the school or college in this

  - Link with the local LSCB to make sure staff are aware of training opportunities and the latest local policies on safeguarding

  - Where children leave the school or college ensure their child protection file is copied for any new school or college as soon as possible but transferred separately from the main pupil file

---

[49] Section 17(10) Children Act 1989: those unlikely to achieve a reasonable standard of health and development without local authority services, those whose health and development is likely to be significantly impaired without the provision of such services, or disabled children.

Annex C: Special circumstances

Boarding schools and children's homes

1.   Children may be particularly vulnerable in residential settings. In reflection of that, there are additional requirements for boarding schools, residential special schools, and children's homes. These are set out in National Minimum Standards for the relevant setting. All schools and colleges that provide such residential accommodation and/or are registered as children's homes must comply with the relevant National Minimum Standards for their sector. Such schools and colleges should be particularly alert to the signs of abuse in such settings and work closely with the host local authority and, where relevant, any local authorities that have placed their children there. The relevant guidance for each sector is on GOV.UK and the relevant links are listed below:

The National Minimum Standards for Boarding Schools

The National Minimum Standards for Residential Special Schools

The National Minimum Standards for Accommodation of Students under 18 by Further Education Colleges

The National Minimum Standards for Children's Homes

Children staying with host families

2.   Schools and colleges quite often make arrangements for their children to have learning experiences where, for short periods, the children may be provided with care and accommodation by a host family to which they are not related. This might happen, for example, but not only, as part of a foreign exchange visit or sports tour. Such arrangements could amount to "private fostering" under the Children Act 1989 or the Safeguarding Vulnerable Groups Act 2006, or both. The following paragraphs are not intended to be a comprehensive guide to all the circumstances in which private fostering may arise, but only to those situations which might arise for schools and colleges through the normal course of their activities in promoting learning activities for children.

3.   Where the child is under the age of 18 and the person who provides the care and accommodation is paid to provide that arrangement, or the arrangement is not made by the child's family, the private fostering arrangement could amount to regulated activity for the purposes of the Safeguarding Vulnerable Groups Act 2006 regardless of the duration of the arrangement.[50] If the school or college is responsible for making the arrangement, and has the power to terminate the arrangement, then it could be the regulated activity

---

[50] Safeguarding Vulnerable Groups Act 2006, Section 53. This also applies to schools and colleges if they broker student accommodation with host families for which the host family receives a payment from a third party, such as a language school. At a future date, the regulated activity provider will have a duty to carry out a barred list check on any new carer – section 34ZA Safeguarding Vulnerable Groups Act 2006.

provider. If the arrangement is made by a third party, such as a language school, and that third party has the power to terminate the arrangement, then the third party is the regulated activity provider. A regulated activity provider will be committing an offence if they knowingly allow a person to carry out a regulated activity whilst barred.[51] Where the school or college is the regulated activity provider, it should request a DBS Certificate with barred list check.

4.   Where schools and colleges have not been involved in making the arrangement but a member of staff or volunteer at a school or college becomes aware that a pupil may be in a private fostering arrangement, where a child under the age of 16 (or 18 if disabled) is provided with care and accommodation by someone to whom they are not related in that person's home, they should raise this in the first instance with the designated senior person for child protection. The school or college should notify the local authority of the circumstances, and the local authority will check that the arrangement is suitable and safe for the child.

5.   A person who is barred from regulated activity will themselves be committing an offence under the Children Act 1989[52] and under the Safeguarding Vulnerable Groups Act 2006[53] if they privately foster a child. If the school or college has any reason to believe that the third party is failing to undertake a statutory duty they should notify the police.

6.   Schools and colleges arranging for their children to stay with families overseas should be aware that the DBS cannot access criminal records held overseas. Host families in other countries, therefore, cannot be checked in the same way by local authorities as schools and colleges in this country when children stay abroad. Schools and colleges should work with partner schools abroad to ensure that similar assurances are undertaken prior to a visit. If they wish, local authorities and schools can contact the relevant foreign embassy or High Commission of the country in question and find out if similar checks can be done in that country.

---

[51] Section 9 Safeguarding Vulnerable Groups Act 2006.
[52] Section 68(3A)(a) Children Act 1989.
[53] Section 7 Safeguarding Vulnerable Groups Act 2006.

Annex D: Statutory guidance – regulated activity (children)

This statutory guidance on the supervision of activity with children which is regulated activity when unsupervised is also published separately on <u>GOV.UK</u>.

1.   This document fulfils the duty in legislation[i,ii] that the Secretary of State must publish statutory guidance on supervision of activity by workers with children, which when unsupervised is regulated activity. This guidance applies in England, Wales and Northern Ireland. It covers settings including but not limited to schools, childcare establishments, colleges, youth groups and sports clubs.

2.   For too long child protection policy has been developed in haste and in response to individual tragedies, with the well-intentioned though misguided belief that every risk could be mitigated and every loophole closed. The pressure has been to prescribe and legislate more. This has led to public confusion, a fearful workforce and a dysfunctional culture of mistrust between children and adults. This Government is taking a different approach.

3.   We start with a presumption of trust and confidence in those who work with children, and the good sense and judgment of their managers. This guidance applies when an organisation decides to supervise with the aim that the supervised work will not be regulated activity (when it would be, if not so supervised). In such a case, the law makes three main points:

- there must be supervision by a person who is in regulated activity[iii];

- the supervision must be regular and day to day; and

- the supervision must be "reasonable in all the circumstances to ensure the protection of children".

The organisation must have regard to this guidance. That gives local managers the flexibility to determine what is reasonable for their circumstances. While the precise nature and level of supervision will vary from case to case, guidance on the main legal points above is as follows.

4.   Supervision by a person in regulated activity/regular and day to day: supervisors must be in regulated activity themselves[iv]. The duty that supervision must take place "on a regular basis" means that supervision must not, for example, be concentrated during the first few weeks of an activity and then tail off thereafter, becoming the exception not the rule. It must take place on an ongoing basis, whether the worker has just started or has been doing the activity for some time.

5.   Reasonable in the circumstances: within the statutory duty, the level of supervision may differ, depending on all the circumstances of a case. Organisations should consider the following factors in deciding the specific level of supervision the organisation will require in an individual case:

- ages of the children, including whether their ages differ widely;

- number of children that the individual is working with;

- whether or not other workers are helping to look after the children;

- the nature of the individual's work (or, in a specified place such as a school, the individual's opportunity for contact with children);

- how vulnerable the children are (the more they are, the more an organisation might opt for workers to be in regulated activity);

- how many workers would be supervised by each supervising worker.

6. In law, an organisation will have no entitlement to do a barred list check on a worker who, because they are supervised, is not in regulated activity.

EXAMPLES

Volunteer, in a specified place

Mr Jones, a new volunteer, helps children with reading at a local school for two mornings a week. Mr Jones is generally based in the classroom, in sight of the teacher. Sometimes Mr Jones takes some of the children to a separate room to listen to them reading, where Mr Jones is supervised by a paid classroom assistant, who is in that room most of the time. The teacher and classroom assistant are in regulated activity. The head teacher decides whether their supervision is such that Mr Jones is not in regulated activity.

Volunteer, not in a specified place

Mr Wood, a new entrant volunteer, assists with the coaching of children at his local cricket club. The children are divided into small groups, with assistant coaches such as Mr Wood assigned to each group. The head coach oversees the coaching, spends time with each of the groups, and has sight of all the groups (and the assistant coaches) for most of the time. The head coach is in regulated activity. The club managers decide whether the coach's supervision is such that Mr Wood is not in regulated activity.

Employee, not in a specified place

Mrs Shah starts as a paid activity assistant at a youth club. She helps to instruct a group of children, and is supervised by the youth club leader who is in regulated activity. The youth club managers decide whether the leader's supervision is such that Mrs Shah is not in regulated activity.

In each example, the organisation uses the following steps when deciding whether a new worker will be supervised to such a level that the new worker is not in regulated activity:

- consider whether the worker is doing work that, if unsupervised, would be regulated activity. If the worker is not, the remaining steps are unnecessary;

- consider whether the worker will be supervised by a person in regulated activity, and whether the supervision will be regular and day to day, bearing in mind paragraph 4 of this guidance;

- consider whether the supervision will be reasonable in all the circumstances to ensure the protection of children, bearing in mind the factors set out in paragraph 5 of this guidance above; and if it is a specified place such as a school:

- consider whether the supervised worker is a volunteer[v].

i Safeguarding Vulnerable Groups Act 2006, amended by Protection of Freedoms Act 2012: Schedule 4, paragraph 5A: guidance must be *"for the purpose of assisting"* organisations *"in deciding whether supervision is of such a kind that"* the supervisee is not in regulated activity.

ii Safeguarding Vulnerable Groups (Northern Ireland) Order 2007, Schedule 2, paragraph 5A, is as above on guidance on "supervision" for Northern Ireland.

iii If the work is in a specified place such as a school, paid workers remain in regulated activity even if supervised.

iv From 2013-14, the Government plans to commence a statutory duty on an organisation arranging regulated activity (under the 2006 Act or 2007 Order, both as amended) to check that a person entering regulated activity is not barred from regulated activity; and plans to commence a stand-alone barring check service by the new Disclosure and Barring Service.

v A volunteer is: in England and Wales, a person who performs an activity which involves spending time, unpaid (except for travel and other approved out-of-pocket expenses), doing something which aims to benefit someone (individuals or groups) other than or in addition to close relatives; in Northern Ireland, a person engaged, or to be engaged, in an activity for a non-profit organisation or person which involves spending time unpaid (except for travel and other approved out-of-pocket expenses) doing something which amounts to a benefit to some third party other than, or in addition to, a close relative.

Annex E: Disclosure and Barring Service checks

These are the types of checks available to those working with children:

Type of check	What the check involves	Positions eligible for this level of check
Standard check	Check of the Police National Computer records of convictions, cautions, reprimands and warnings.	The position being applied for must be covered by an exempted question in the Rehabilitation of Offenders Act 1974 (Exceptions) Order 1975.
Enhanced check	Check of the Police National Computer records **plus** other information held by police such as interviews and allegations. This information must be relevant to the sector and be approved by the police for inclusion on the certificate.	The position being applied for must be covered by an exempted question in both the Rehabilitation of Offenders Act 1974 (Exceptions) Order 1975 and in Part 5 of the Police Act 1997 (Criminal Records) Regulations.*
Enhanced criminal record check with children's and/or adult's barred list information	Check of the Police National Computer records **plus** other information held by police **plus** check of the DBS Children's Barred List **plus** check of the DBS Adults' Barred List.	The position must be eligible for an enhanced level criminal record check as above and be for a purpose listed in Regulation 5 of the Police Act 1997 (Criminal Records) Regulations* as able to check the barred list(s).

*This legislation does not provide a list of job roles that are eligible for this check – such a list does not exist. Instead, the Rehabilitation of Offenders Act 1974 (Exceptions) Order 1975 sets out the 'exempted questions' for which a standard check can be obtained. Similarly, the Police Act 1997 (Criminal Records) Regulations 2002 set out the purposes for which an enhanced check can be obtained, and the Police Act 1997 (Criminal Records) (No 2) Regulations 2009 list the circumstances in which an enhanced check will automatically include a barred list check. It is important to note that the Regulations can also remove roles, duties or activities through the removal of an exempted question or of a particular purpose. The Rehabilitation of Offenders Act 1974 (Exceptions) Order 1975, the Police Act 1997 (Criminal Records) Regulations 2002 and the Police Act 1997 (Criminal Records) (No 2) Regulations 2009 can all be found on www.legislation.gov.uk

The basic criminal record check can be undertaken on any applicant for work which does not involve working with children. Currently, this service is available to any employer and self-employed people anywhere in the UK but it must be requested through Disclosure Scotland. The DBS plans to offer basic criminal record checks in the future.